What Really Matters?

Redefining Time Management

Hope Grace
PUBLISHING

Alexandria, Virginia, USA

By **Hope Grace**

Copyright Page

Published by Hope Grace Publishing
Alexandria, VA, USA

ISBN: 978-1-966423-30-0 Paperback
ISBN: 978-1-966423-32-4 Hardback
ISBN: 978-1-966423-33-1 eBook

Library of Congress Control Number: 2025900451

This is a work of nonfiction. All events and experiences described in this book are based on the author's personal life. Any resemblance to persons, living or dead, other than those explicitly mentioned, is purely coincidental.

For permissions or inquiries, contact:
HopeGracePublishing.com

Contents

Introduction: Redefining Time Management

The purpose of *What Really Matters? — Redefining Time Management* is to spotlight the overlooked yet essential priorities that often slip through the cracks in our busy lives. These priorities — moments of connection, lessons in financial discipline, or reflections on legacy — may seem simple, but their impact can ripple through generations. By examining each stage of life, this book aims to help you identify those critical but often-missed opportunities to live intentionally and meaningfully.

We'll journey through life's phases — from childhood to later years — exploring what truly matters at each stage, whether it's spending time with children beyond the basics of parenting, helping young adults envision a career path and save for the future, or focusing on relationships and legacy in later years. This isn't a comprehensive guide to time management; it's a focused exploration of priorities that make life deeply meaningful.

A Personal Reflection

I once thought time management was about doing more. I'd fill my days with tasks and obligations, believing that productivity equated to success. One evening, as I rushed to finish some work, my young son asked me to join him for a computer game. I told him, "I don't have time." At that time, I was an underemployed single mom attending college. He didn't insist, and I felt relieved. Many years later, when he was in high school, he complained, "You don't love me. You are only fulfilling your responsibilities." At that time, I was a full-time application developer and systems analyst while pursuing a master's degree in Information Science. I dismissed his complaint as nonsense.

After he went to college, I eventually realized what I had missed. I wish somebody had written a book like this, and I had been lucky enough to read it. My heart still aches whenever I recall those dismissed moments.

That experience taught me a valuable lesson: Time isn't just a resource to manage; it's a canvas on which we paint the story of our lives. And the most beautiful parts of that story come from focusing on what really matters.

This book is my attempt to share that lesson with you. Together, let's redefine time management and create a life centered on love, purpose, and meaning.

Part 1: Foundational Insights on Time and Priorities

Chapter 1: The Gift of Time

Time is the most precious resource we have.

Unlike money, possessions, or even health, time is

finite and irreplaceable. Once a moment passes, it is

gone forever. This reality makes time both a gift and

a challenge. How we use it determines the quality

and meaning of our lives.

The Finite Nature of Time

Each of us is given 24 hours in a day, 168 hours

in a week, and, if we are fortunate, decades of life.

Yet, no matter how much time we have, it always

feels fleeting. This sense of scarcity forces us to

make choices about how we spend our days. Every

"yes" to one activity is a "no" to countless others.

Recognizing this trade-off is the first step toward

valuing time as the precious gift it is.

Urgent vs. Important

Not all demands on our time are created equal. The distinction between what is urgent and what is truly important is critical to living a meaningful life. Urgent tasks scream for our attention — emails, deadlines, or minor crises — but they often lack lasting significance. Important tasks, on the other hand, align with our deepest values and long-term goals. They include nurturing relationships, pursuing personal growth, and contributing to something larger than ourselves.

Learning to prioritize the important over the urgent requires intentionality. It means stepping back to assess whether our daily actions align with what we value most. It may also mean saying "no" to distractions or obligations that pull us away from our priorities.

Aligning Time with Values

A meaningful life isn't about how much we do but about doing the right things. When we align our use of time with our values, we experience greater fulfillment and purpose. This alignment doesn't happen by accident. It requires reflection, clarity, and the courage to make choices that honor what matters most.

Consider this: How would you spend your time if you knew you had only one year to live? While this question may seem morbid, it clarifies what truly matters. Few of us would prioritize work emails or trivial tasks. Instead, we would focus on love, connection, and the pursuits that bring us joy and meaning.

By treating time as the gift it is, we can make choices that enrich our lives and the lives of those around us. The chapters that follow will explore how to identify and act on these priorities at each stage of life. But first, let's reflect on this foundational truth: Time is precious. Use it wisely, and it becomes the greatest gift of all.

Do You Have Time? A Deeper Look at What It Means

"Do you have time?" is a question we hear often. At first glance, it seems simple. But have you ever stopped to think about what it really means? And more importantly, what your response conveys?

When someone asks this question, we often reply with another question: "For what?" This instinctive response reflects an underlying truth — our time is finite, and how we allocate it depends on what we deem important. After all, every one of us has the same 24 hours in a day, 7 days in a week, 52 weeks in a year. The difference lies in how we prioritize

and value the moments we have.

The True Meaning Behind "Do You Have Time?"

Let's reconsider this exchange:

- **Person A**: "Do you have time?"
- **Person B**: "For what?"
- **Person A**: "I'm thinking of taking a walk after dinner."
- **Person B**: "Sure."

On the surface, this seems straightforward. But if

we reframe the conversation, it reveals something

deeper:

- **Person A**: "Are you available?"
- **Person B**: "It depends on the importance of the matter."
- **Person A**: "I'd like to take a walk after dinner."
- **Person B**: "I'd love to spend time with you on a walk after dinner."

In this rephrased version, the focus shifts from merely allocating time to expressing intent and priorities. The act of saying "yes" becomes more than a passive agreement — it becomes a statement of value and connection.

Time Management is About Priorities

Every time we say, "I don't have time," what we're really saying is, "This is not a priority for me right now." It's not about the number of hours in the day but about how we choose to spend them.

For example, if you decline a request to meet, it isn't just a matter of being busy. It's a matter of deciding that something else — be it work, rest, or another obligation — takes precedence.

This is not inherently wrong. We all have responsibilities and limits. However, understanding what our "no" communicates can lead to more thoughtful decisions. The next time you say you don't have time, consider what you're really saying: "I don't have time for you. I have more important things to do."

Prioritizing Relationships

When we consciously prioritize relationships, even mundane activities like a post-dinner walk become meaningful. Saying "yes" isn't just about being available — it's about choosing to connect.

Time management, at its core, isn't about squeezing more into our day. It's about aligning our actions with what matters most to us. And often, what matters most isn't just tasks or deadlines — it's people.

Chapter 2: Less Is More — Focusing on the Essentials

In a world that glorifies busyness, the idea of doing less can feel counterintuitive. We often equate a packed schedule with productivity and success, but is it really the best way to live? The truth is, time management isn't about cramming more into each day. It's about making room for what truly matters. By focusing on quality rather than quantity, we can achieve a more meaningful and fulfilling life.

Quality Over Quantity

The key to effective time management isn't doing everything — it's doing the right things. Prioritizing quality over quantity means dedicating your time and energy to the activities, relationships, and goals that align with your core values. This might mean saying "no" more often, scaling back commitments, or intentionally carving out time for rest and reflection.

Consider this: A single heartfelt conversation with a loved one can be more impactful than a dozen superficial interactions. Similarly, spending an hour deeply focused on an important project can yield better results than a day spent multitasking. When we focus on quality, we maximize the value of our time.

Identifying Overlooked Priorities

The demands of modern life often cause us to overlook the priorities that truly make a difference. What are the things that, if neglected, could lead to regret later on? Some examples might include:

- **Relationships**: Spending meaningful time with family and friends rather than simply being in the same space.
- **Health**: Making time for exercise, sleep, and mental well-being.
- **Personal Growth**: Pursuing hobbies, education, or spiritual practices that bring joy and purpose.

By identifying these overlooked priorities, we can make deliberate choices to integrate them into our lives. It's not about doing more — it's about doing what matters most.

The Dangers of Distractions and Obligations

Distractions are the enemy of focus and intentionality. From endless notifications to the constant pull of social media, it's easy to let trivial things consume our attention. These distractions not only waste time but also rob us of the ability to be fully present in our lives.

Unnecessary obligations are another major obstacle. It's tempting to say "yes" to every invitation, request, or opportunity that comes our way. But overcommitting can leave us feeling stretched thin and unable to give our best to the things that matter most.

Learning to say "no" is a crucial skill for focusing on the essentials. It's not about being selfish — it's about being intentional. When we free ourselves from distractions and unnecessary obligations, we create space for what truly matters.

Simplify to Amplify

The beauty of focusing on the essentials is that it simplifies our lives while amplifying their meaning. By doing less, we free ourselves to experience more — more connection, more joy, more fulfillment. The path to a meaningful life isn't about adding; it's about subtracting. It's about letting go of the things that don't matter so we can focus on the things that do.

As you move forward, ask yourself: What truly deserves my time and energy? What can I let go of to make room for what matters most? By embracing the principle that less is more, you'll begin to live a life that is not only productive but deeply meaningful.

Part 2: Time and Priorities Across Life Stages

Chapter 3: Childhood — More Than Responsibilities

Childhood is a fleeting stage, yet its impact lasts a lifetime. For parents, this time is often filled with obligations: providing meals, ensuring safety, helping with schoolwork, and more. While these responsibilities are essential, they represent the bare minimum of what children truly need. Beyond fulfilling obligations, spending quality time with children — more than what is "necessary" — is critical to making them feel deeply loved and secure.

The Overlooked Importance of Extra Time

Parents often feel stretched thin, balancing work, household duties, and myriad responsibilities. It can be tempting to think, "I've done enough; they'll understand." But children don't just need their parents to meet their physical and logistical needs — they need presence, attention, and connection.

This realization hit me hard when I reflected on my own journey as a mother. I believed I was doing my best and others seemed to agree. I provided for my son, ensured he was cared for, helped him with college applications, provided guidance for his career, and started his retirement savings with his first paycheck from Burger King during high school. While these efforts demonstrated care and support, they were not enough to convey the emotional presence my son needed most. Practical help is important, but it cannot replace the deep connection that comes from being truly present in a child's life.

Looking back, I see the moments I missed, the times I focused on responsibilities rather than connection, and it fills me with regret. I failed at the most important role — being a loving mom. My son's words still echo in my heart: "You don't love me. You are only fulfilling your responsibilities." At the time, I dismissed his words as ungratefulness, but now I understand their weight. While practical guidance and financial planning were valuable, what he truly needed was for me to be present, to share in his joys and struggles with undivided attention.

Time spent beyond what is strictly necessary sends a powerful message: "You matter to me. You're worth my time." These moments create a foundation of love and trust that supports children as they grow. The extra time doesn't need to be extravagant or time-consuming; it simply needs to be intentional.

How Quality Time Builds Security and Love

Children perceive love not only through words but also through actions. When you invest your time in them, you're showing that they are valued and prioritized. This sense of security allows children to thrive emotionally and mentally.

Quality time fosters open communication, enabling children to share their thoughts, fears, and joys without fear of judgment. It strengthens the parent-child bond and lays the groundwork for a relationship built on trust and understanding. These connections often translate into better emotional resilience, higher self-esteem, and stronger interpersonal relationships as they grow.

Practical Ways to Create Moments of Connection

Modern life can feel overwhelming, making it difficult to carve out meaningful time with children. However, even small, intentional efforts can make a big difference:

1. **Be Fully Present**: Put away distractions like phones and laptops during one-on-one time. Even 15 minutes of undivided attention can leave a lasting impact.
2. **Create Rituals**: Establish regular routines that encourage bonding, such as bedtime stories, family dinners, or a weekly walk in the park.
3. **Share Interests**: Engage in activities that your child enjoys, whether it's playing a game, crafting, or exploring their favorite hobbies together.
4. **Involve Them in Your Day**: Turn everyday tasks into opportunities to connect. Cooking dinner, gardening, or running errands can become special moments when done together.
5. **Listen Actively**: When your child speaks, listen with genuine interest. Reflect back what you hear to show them they're truly understood.

The Ripple Effect of Quality Time

The time and effort invested in childhood have far-reaching effects. While practical support such as career guidance and financial planning is valuable, it must be complemented by emotional presence. Children who feel deeply loved and secure are more likely to develop into confident, compassionate, and well-adjusted adults. They carry the lessons of love and connection into their own relationships, creating a ripple effect that extends far beyond their childhood. Practical efforts alone do not suffice if they lack the emotional presence children need most. Our children are the ultimate judge of whether we have been good parents.

As parents, we have the power to shape not only the lives of our children but also the world they will impact. By prioritizing quality time, we honor the profound responsibility and privilege of parenthood. The gift of time—given freely and with love—is one of the greatest legacies we can leave for our children.

Chapter 4: Early Adulthood — Laying a Strong Foundation

Early adulthood is a time of exploration and transformation. For many, it marks the beginning of independence and responsibility, where decisions made can set the trajectory for the rest of their lives. Helping young adults lay a strong foundation during this critical stage involves instilling habits and values that will serve them for decades to come.

Teaching the Importance of Retirement Savings

One of the most impactful lessons to teach young adults is the value of starting retirement savings with their very first paycheck. While retirement may seem a distant concern, the power of compound growth makes early contributions invaluable. For example, a modest investment in a retirement account at age 18 can grow exponentially by the time they reach retirement age, far outpacing contributions made later in life.

This isn't just about numbers — it's about instilling financial discipline. Encouraging young adults to allocate even a small portion of their earnings to savings teaches them to prioritize their future. It also builds confidence and independence, empowering them to take control of their financial destiny.

The Power of Compound Growth and Financial Discipline

Compound growth is one of the most powerful financial tools available. Simply put, it's the process by which investments generate earnings, and those earnings, in turn, generate additional earnings. The earlier someone starts, the more time their money has to grow, making each dollar invested in early adulthood significantly more impactful than dollars invested later.

For example:

- An 18-year-old who invests $100 a month until age 65 will accumulate far more wealth than someone who starts investing $200 a month at age 35.

This simple math highlights the critical importance of starting early. Beyond financial benefits, this habit fosters discipline and helps young adults understand the value of consistency and patience in achieving long-term goals.

Envisioning Long-Term Career Goals

Early adulthood is also a time to envision a meaningful and purposeful career. While some may feel pressured to immediately find their "dream job," it's important to focus on building skills, gaining experience, and understanding personal values. Encourage young adults to ask themselves:

- What motivates me?
- What skills do I want to develop?
- How can I contribute meaningfully to the world?

For example, my son, who loves video games, initially didn't want to go to college and instead wanted to work as a salesperson at a game store after high school. I analyzed the situation with him, pointing out that he would likely earn minimum wage at the game store, which would barely cover his bills. To afford video games, he might need a second job or work long hours, leaving him with little time to actually play them. This practical analysis helped me persuade him to consider college as a path to getting a well-paying job that would enable him to afford video games and enjoy playing them after work. By framing the decision around his passion, I was able to guide him toward a more stable and fulfilling future.

Helping young adults answer these questions can guide them in crafting a career path aligned with their passions and strengths. It's also an opportunity to emphasize that career paths are rarely linear and that adapting to new opportunities is a vital skill.

Practical Guidance for Parents and Mentors

1. **Introduce Financial Literacy**: Teach young adults how to budget, invest, and understand the basics of taxes and retirement accounts. For more detailed strategies on saving and investing early, refer to the book *Simple Strategy to Save $1M in Retirement* in Self-Help Series by Hope Grace.
2. **Set an Example**: Share your own experiences with savings and career planning, highlighting both successes and mistakes.
3. **Encourage Goal Setting**: Help them articulate both short-term and long-term goals, whether financial, personal, or professional.

4. **Provide Resources**: Offer tools like budgeting apps, books on personal finance, or connections to mentors in their field of interest.
5. **Support Exploration**: Encourage them to try different jobs, internships, or volunteer opportunities to discover their interests and strengths.

The Lasting Impact of a Strong Foundation

The habits and perspectives formed in early adulthood have a ripple effect throughout life. By teaching young adults the importance of saving early, fostering financial discipline, and encouraging purposeful career planning, we empower them to build lives of stability, growth, and meaning. These lessons not only benefit the individual but also have the potential to influence future generations, creating a legacy of wisdom and preparation.

As we guide young adults through this transformative stage, we offer them tools to not only succeed but to thrive — helping them lay a foundation strong enough to support their dreams for decades to come.

Chapter 5: Midlife — Balancing and Reassessing

Midlife often feels like a juggling act. It's a time when careers are in full swing, family responsibilities remain significant, and personal aspirations may be pushed to the sidelines. For many, it's also a period of reflection and reevaluation. Are we spending our time on what truly matters? Have our priorities shifted, and are we making space for those changes?

This chapter explores how to reassess priorities during midlife and strike a balance that allows for growth, fulfillment, and meaningful connections.

Reevaluating Priorities

Midlife offers an opportunity to pause and take stock. For me, this reflection began in the month when I turned 50, as I was hit by "50 shoulder," a popular Chinese phrase for "frozen shoulder." I had never imagined something like this would happen to me, especially in the very month I reached this milestone age. I had lived a very healthy life, exercised daily, maintained perfect shape, and always felt full of energy. Despite the passage of time and growing older, I had never felt "old" and thought I would stay forever young.

But when I suddenly couldn't even raise my arm, I was forced to reassess the exercises I had been practicing daily. Most exercise videos available at the time were made by young people in their 20s or 30s, which inspired me to seek movements better suited for my body's changing needs. When I discovered a video teaching "8 Precious Movements," I decided to learn and adapt it for my routine. To make it more convenient for myself, I created an exercise video that I could follow daily. This video is now available on my YouTube channel, "Age Gracefully with Hope" Fitness Channel, where I share exercises that have helped me age gracefully. I still practice this routine almost every day.

This period of adjustment reminded me that reevaluating priorities isn't just about relationships or career; it also involves listening to our bodies and adapting to their needs. Taking time to reflect can provide clarity and direction.

Avoiding the Trap of Busyness

Busyness has become a badge of honor in modern life. Packed schedules and endless to-do lists often create the illusion of productivity, but they can come at a cost. Midlife is an ideal time to challenge this mindset and prioritize quality over quantity.

Focusing on relationships and health is a powerful antidote to the trap of busyness. Meaningful connections with family and friends nurture emotional well-being, while investing in physical and mental health ensures vitality for years to come. Practical steps include:

- Scheduling regular check-ins with loved ones — whether a weekly family dinner or a monthly coffee with a close friend.
- Making physical activity a non-negotiable part of the day.
- Practicing mindfulness or meditation to stay present amid life's demands.

Letting Go of Unnecessary Commitments

One of the most liberating aspects of midlife is the ability to let go of what no longer serves us.

This might mean stepping back from social

obligations, rethinking career ambitions, or simplifying daily routines. Letting go creates space for the things that truly matter.

To identify unnecessary commitments, consider:

- **Assessing Your Calendar**: Review your schedule and ask whether each activity aligns with your priorities.
- **Learning to Say No**: Practice declining requests that don't contribute to your goals or values.
- **Delegating Tasks**: If possible, delegate responsibilities at work or home to free up time and energy.

The Freedom to Pursue Meaningful Goals

By reassessing priorities and shedding unnecessary commitments, midlife can become a time of renewal. It's an opportunity to rediscover passions, deepen relationships, and invest in personal growth. Whether it's learning a new skill, volunteering for a cause, or simply spending more time with family, the freedom to focus on what matters most is one of midlife's greatest gifts.

As you navigate this stage of life, remember that balance isn't about perfection — it's about making intentional choices that align with your values and bring a sense of purpose. By doing so, you can transform midlife into a period of fulfillment and joy, setting the stage for a meaningful future.

Chapter 6: Later Life — Creating a Legacy

Later life brings a unique perspective. With decades of experience behind us, it's a time to reflect on what truly matters and focus on leaving a legacy that extends beyond material success. For me, this stage has also been an opportunity to share my reflections and lessons through writing. I have written a memoir and three self-help books, and this is my fourth book in the self-help series. In this stage of life, priorities often shift toward relationships, wisdom, and contribution — the things that create lasting impact.

Instead of accumulating possessions, consider accumulating memories and connections. Spending quality time with loved ones, sharing stories, and offering guidance are some of the most meaningful ways to use this stage of life. By prioritizing what truly matters, we can create a legacy that reflects our values and enriches the lives of those around us.

Sharing Life Lessons with the Next Generation

One of the most significant contributions we can make in later life is passing on our wisdom. Whether through storytelling, mentorship, or simply being present, sharing life lessons helps guide and inspire the next generation. Practical ways to do this include:

- **Documenting Stories**: Write or record memories, family history, or important lessons you've learned over the years.
- **Mentorship**: Offer guidance to younger family members, friends, or community members navigating similar challenges you've faced.
- **Leading by Example**: Demonstrate values such as kindness, resilience, and generosity in everyday actions.

These efforts ensure that your experiences and insights continue to have an impact long after you're gone.

Prioritizing Presence Over Possessions

In a world focused on material accumulation, later life presents an opportunity to redefine what we leave behind. Possessions, while useful, often pale in comparison to the value of being fully present with loved ones. Prioritizing presence means:

- **Spending Time Together**: Regular visits, phone calls, or shared activities strengthen bonds and create cherished memories.
- **Active Listening**: Engage in meaningful conversations, showing genuine interest in the thoughts and feelings of others.
- **Being Available**: Offer your time and attention, whether it's helping with daily tasks or providing emotional support.

By prioritizing presence, we remind our loved ones that they matter more than any material inheritance.

Building a Legacy of Love and Contribution

A meaningful legacy isn't defined by wealth or possessions — it's measured by the love and contributions we leave behind. Consider ways to contribute to your community, such as volunteering, supporting causes you care about, or creating programs that align with your values.

Legacy-building also involves being intentional about the memories and values you impart. Reflect on questions like:

- How do I want to be remembered?
- What lessons or values do I hope to pass on?
- What impact can I make today that will resonate in the future?

Embracing Later Life with Purpose

Later life is not just a conclusion; it's a culmination. It's a time to celebrate the journey, share what you've learned, and focus on what truly matters. By prioritizing relationships, wisdom, and contribution, you can create a legacy that reflects the best of who you are and inspires others to live with purpose and love.

As we embrace this stage of life, let us remember that the greatest legacies are built not on what we acquire, but on what we give. The love, lessons, and presence we offer today will shape the lives of those we touch for generations to come.

Part 3: Practical Strategies for a Meaningful Life

Chapter 7: Time Alignment Tools

Time is our most valuable resource, yet it's easy to spend it on activities that don't align with our true priorities. How often do we reach the end of the day feeling exhausted but unfulfilled, wondering where our time went? To live a meaningful life, we must ensure our time aligns with what matters most. This chapter explores practical tools and strategies to help evaluate and realign how you spend your time.

Evaluating Time Alignment

The first step in aligning your time with your priorities is understanding where it currently goes. Start by reflecting on these questions:

- **What are my top priorities?** Think about the relationships, goals, and values that matter most to you.
- **How much time do I currently dedicate to these priorities?** Be honest with yourself about whether they receive the attention they deserve.
- **What activities consume the majority of my time?** Identify time-wasting habits or obligations that don't serve your goals.
- **Am I satisfied with how I'm spending my time?** If not, what changes would make you feel more aligned and fulfilled?

Tracking your time for a week can provide valuable insights. Use a journal, app, or spreadsheet to document how you spend each hour. At the end of the week, compare your time log to your priorities. Are they in sync? If not, it's time to make adjustments.

Tools for Focusing on Quality Interactions and Essential Goals

Once you've evaluated your time alignment, the next step is to implement tools that help you focus on what truly matters. Here are some practical options:

1. Time Blocking

Time blocking involves scheduling specific blocks of time for different activities. This method ensures that your priorities have dedicated space in your day. For example:

- Block time for family dinners or one-on-one time with loved ones.
- Set aside focused work periods free from distractions.
- Schedule regular self-care or exercise sessions.

By assigning time to your most important activities, you reduce the risk of neglecting them amid daily chaos.

2. The Eisenhower Matrix

This tool helps you prioritize tasks based on urgency and importance:

- **Urgent and Important**: Handle these tasks immediately.
- **Important but Not Urgent**: Schedule these for later and focus on them proactively.
- **Urgent but Not Important**: Delegate these tasks if possible.
- **Neither Urgent nor Important**: Eliminate these to free up time for what matters.

Using this matrix encourages intentional decision-making and prevents wasting time on low-value activities.

3. The Two-Minute Rule

If a task takes less than two minutes to complete, do it immediately. This simple rule prevents small tasks from piling up and consuming mental energy later.

4. The Pareto Principle (80/20 Rule)

This principle suggests that 80% of results come from 20% of efforts. Identify the 20% of activities that yield the greatest impact and focus your time there.

5. Mindfulness Practices

Mindfulness helps you stay present and fully engaged in each moment. Whether it's a conversation with a loved one or completing a work project, being mindful ensures you make the most of your time.

Realigning Time with Priorities

Once you've identified and implemented these tools, periodically reassess your time alignment. Life changes, and so do priorities. Regular reflection ensures you stay on track and continue to use your time intentionally.

- Set aside a monthly or quarterly review to evaluate your time and adjust as needed.

- Ask yourself: Are my actions reflecting my values? What adjustments can I make to improve alignment?

Final Thoughts

Time alignment isn't about perfection; it's about intentionality. By regularly evaluating how you spend your time and using tools to focus on quality and essentials, you can ensure your days are filled with purpose and fulfillment. In doing so, you'll create a life that truly reflects your values and priorities.

Chapter 8: Saying Yes and No with Purpose

In a world full of opportunities and obligations, the ability to say "yes" and "no" with purpose is essential to living a meaningful life. Every decision we make about where to invest our time and energy shapes our priorities and impacts our overall well-being. This chapter explores how to evaluate what deserves your commitment and offers strategies for confidently saying no to distractions and less meaningful activities.

Deciding What Deserves Your Time and Energy

Not everything that demands your time is worth your attention. To determine what truly deserves your commitment, consider the following:

- **Does it align with my values?** Reflect on whether the opportunity or request aligns with your core beliefs and goals.
- **What is the long-term impact?** Think about whether this choice contributes to your growth, relationships, or purpose.
- **Am I saying yes out of obligation or desire?** Be honest about whether your decision stems from genuine interest or external pressure.
- **What will I need to sacrifice?** Consider the trade-offs. Saying yes often means saying no to something else that may matter more.

Taking a moment to reflect before committing ensures your "yes" is intentional and meaningful.

The Power of Saying No

Saying no can feel uncomfortable, especially when it involves turning down people or opportunities that seem worthwhile. However, every time you say yes to something that doesn't align with your priorities, you're saying no to something else — potentially something far more important.

Learning to say no isn't about rejecting others;

it's about honoring your values and boundaries.

Here are some key strategies to help:

1. Be Honest and Direct

When you need to say no, do so with honesty

and kindness. For example:

- "Thank you for thinking of me, but I can't commit to this right now."
- "I appreciate the opportunity, but I need to focus on my existing priorities."

Being clear and respectful avoids

misunderstandings and maintains relationships.

2. Use the "Pause and Evaluate" Method

Instead of agreeing immediately, give yourself

time to think. Say:

- "Let me check my schedule and get back to you."

This allows you to evaluate whether the request aligns with your priorities without the pressure of an immediate response.

3. Set Boundaries in Advance

Establishing clear boundaries helps you avoid overcommitment. For example:

- Block specific times for family, self-care, or focused work and treat them as non-negotiable.
- Let others know your general availability and limits, such as: "I'm happy to help during work hours, but I reserve evenings for family time."

4. Offer Alternatives

If you want to help but can't fully commit, suggest alternatives:

- "I can't join the committee, but I'd be happy to help with one project."
- "I don't have the time to meet this week, but we could catch up over the phone."

Providing options shows goodwill while respecting your boundaries.

Reframing "No" as a Positive

Saying no isn't about shutting doors; it's about opening space for the things that matter most. By reframing no as a tool for intentional living, you can:

- Protect your time and energy for meaningful pursuits.
- Reduce stress and prevent burnout.
- Deepen your commitment to the relationships and goals that truly matter.

Final Thoughts

Every yes and no shapes the story of your life. By deciding what deserves your time and energy and confidently saying no to distractions, you create room for the things that bring fulfillment and purpose. Remember, saying no is not a rejection of others; it's a commitment to yourself and the life you want to lead.

Chapter 9: Living Intentionally Every Day

Living intentionally is about aligning your daily actions with what truly matters. It's a commitment to prioritize the people, goals, and values that bring meaning to your life. While this may seem like a lofty ideal, it can be achieved through simple, consistent habits that keep your focus on key priorities as life evolves. This chapter explores how to incorporate intentionality into your everyday life.

Simple Habits for Intentional Living

Small, consistent actions can have a profound impact over time. Here are some simple habits to help ensure your daily life reflects your priorities:

1. Start Your Day with Reflection

Begin each morning by setting an intention. Ask yourself:

- What is the most important thing I want to accomplish today?
- How can I make time for what truly matters?
- Who needs my attention and care today?

Writing these intentions down can help you stay focused and grounded throughout the day.

2. Practice Gratitude

Take a few moments each day to reflect on what you're grateful for. This practice shifts your mindset to positivity and helps you recognize the value in your relationships, achievements, and experiences.

3. Review and Adjust Your Schedule

Regularly review your schedule to ensure it aligns with your priorities. Use tools like time blocking or weekly planning to dedicate space for meaningful activities, such as spending time with loved ones, pursuing personal growth, or working toward long-term goals.

4. Limit Distractions

Identify and minimize distractions that pull you away from intentional living. Whether it's limiting screen time, reducing unnecessary commitments, or creating boundaries, small adjustments can free up time and energy for what matters most.

5. End Your Day with Reflection

Conclude your day by reviewing your actions. Ask yourself:

- Did I spend my time on what truly matters?
- What did I learn today?
- How can I improve tomorrow?

This habit fosters continuous growth and ensures you remain aligned with your values.

Maintaining Focus as Life Evolves

Life is dynamic, and priorities shift over time. To maintain focus, it's essential to periodically reassess your goals and values. Here's how:

1. Schedule Regular Check-Ins

Set aside time monthly, quarterly, or annually to evaluate your life's direction. Reflect on questions like:

- Are my current actions aligned with my long-term goals?
- Have my priorities changed?
- What adjustments can I make to better reflect my values?

2. Embrace Flexibility

Intentional living doesn't mean rigidly adhering to a plan. Be open to adapting as circumstances change, ensuring your actions remain aligned with what matters most.

3. Seek Support and Accountability

Share your goals and intentions with trusted friends or family members. Their encouragement and feedback can help you stay focused and motivated.

The Ripple Effect of Intentional Living

Living intentionally every day creates a ripple effect that extends beyond your own life. By aligning your actions with your values, you inspire others to do the same. Your intentional choices strengthen relationships, foster personal growth, and contribute to a life filled with purpose and fulfillment.

Final Thoughts

Intentional living is not about perfection; it's about progress. By cultivating simple habits and maintaining focus as life evolves, you can ensure your days reflect what truly matters. Remember, the most meaningful life isn't one filled with endless achievements but one rooted in love, purpose, and intentionality. Start today, and let your daily actions shape the legacy you wish to leave.

Conclusion: A Call to Focus on What Matters Most

As we navigate life's journey, it becomes increasingly clear that meaning is not found in grand gestures or endless achievements. Instead, it emerges from the small, intentional choices we make every day. These choices — how we spend our time, the relationships we nurture, the goals we pursue — define who we are and the legacy we leave behind.

Throughout this book, we've explored how to identify and focus on what truly matters at every stage of life. From childhood to later years, the essence of a meaningful life remains constant: prioritizing love, growth, and contribution. By aligning our actions with these values, we create a life of purpose and fulfillment.

Living with Purpose

Living with purpose doesn't require perfection. It's about progress, intention, and learning along the way. Each day offers an opportunity to:

- Choose connection over distraction.
- Focus on quality over quantity.
- Invest in relationships, health, and personal growth.

When we center our lives on what matters most, we not only enrich our own experience but also inspire others to do the same. Our actions ripple outward, touching the lives of those around us and creating a positive impact that extends beyond our immediate reach.

Building a Legacy

Legacy is not measured by material wealth or accolades but by the love, wisdom, and values we pass on. By living intentionally and prioritizing what truly matters, we ensure that our legacy reflects the best of who we are. Whether it's the lessons we teach, the kindness we show, or the time we dedicate to those we care about, our legacy is built moment by moment, choice by choice.

A Final Invitation

As you close this book, I invite you to take a moment to reflect. What truly matters to you? How can you align your daily actions with your deepest values? What small, intentional choices can you make today to live with purpose and create a meaningful legacy?

Remember, the journey of a meaningful life is not about doing more — it's about focusing on what matters most. By prioritizing love, growth, and legacy, you can shape a life that reflects your values and inspires others to live with intention.

Let today be the beginning of that journey.

Choose what matters most, and let your actions tell

the story of a life well-lived.

About the Author

Hope Grace is an author, translator, and storyteller whose work bridges the realms of identity, faith, and personal growth. Born in China and now an accomplished Senior IT Security Analyst in the United States, Hope brings a unique perspective shaped by her journey as an immigrant, a single mother, and a Christian advocate.

With a BA in Philosophy from Peking University, a Divinity degree, and an MS in Information Science, Hope combines intellectual curiosity with heartfelt storytelling. She uses her pen name, Hope Grace, to inspire others to embrace courage, purpose, and authenticity in every aspect of life.

In addition to her literary achievements, Hope Grace has a passion for empowering others through reflections on faith, relationships, and financial

independence. Her self-help series, including *From*

Passive to Passion: A Chinese Immigrant's Journey

to American Activism, is a testament to her belief in

transformation through action.

Through her imprint, Hope Grace Publishing,

she continues to champion voices that matter and

share stories that resonate deeply with readers

worldwide.

www.ingramcontent.com/pod-product-compliance
Lightning Source LLC
Chambersburg PA
CBHW032103020426
42335CB00011B/465